MW01171832

HERE'S THE THING ABOUT IT...

A Memoir
by Hal Stein

Printed in the U.S.A. by CreateSpace, Charleston, SC

Here's the Thing About It...
Authored by Harold Gene Stein
Photographs provided by Harold Stein & Family
Edited by Jane Brandi Johnson
Cover design by Lisa Bohart, illustrator
Layout and pre-press production by MJ Clark

ISBN-13: 978-1719215749
ISBN-10: 171921574X

Library of Congress Control Number:
BISAC: Adult Biography / Memoir / Historical

DEDICATION FROM HAL STEIN

My Legacy

When one thinks about how they want to live their life, I think I found it all in the Scout's Law when I was 12 years old. This Law served me well throughout my life, and I made a point of taking it seriously. It is certainly a good place to start for anyone who needs a path for life. *A Scout is trustworthy, loyal, helpful, friendly, courteous, kind, obedient, cheerful, thrifty, brave, clean, and reverent.*

The purpose of this book is to leave a written legacy for my children, grandchildren, and great-grandchildren who may not know me as well as I would have liked.

I want to tell them how much I love them. *This is the best way I know!*

EDITOR'S NOTE

Hal Stein vividly presents a lifetime of adventure from childhood to present day, in his book of memoirs entitled, **Here's the Thing About It...** *After his mother's untimely death when he was six years old, Hal quickly learned that a positive approach to life was the most productive way to carry on. He found an abundance of encouragement from loving neighbors and family who showed him that it does take a "village" to raise a happy and healthy child. Not many people can say that they learned how to triumph over adversity by their seventh birthday!*

Here's the Thing About It... *is a testimony that children, when given love and fair opportunity, will embrace the many joys of growing up - even in difficult situations. It is a portrait of education, good times, hard work, changes, family, faith, and friendship. It is also a dedication to Hal's future generations: His wish is for each and every one of you to live a full life with an open heart.*

- Jane B. Johnson

Table of Contents

1

The Steins

A look back at my father's parents

My grandpa, Aaron Stein, was born in Bucharest, Romania in 1875. My grandmother, Sarah Weiner Stein, was a Latvian orphan from the capital city of Riga. Her birth year is estimated to be 1876. Both Aaron and Sarah came to America through Ellis Island. Both had a sort of job offer or promise of work in the city of Chicago, so they left their respective countries with hope for a better life in a new country. From the historical knowledge of Ellis Island, we know that Aaron and Sarah must have traveled to America sometime after the year (1892) when European immigrants were initially welcomed. Grover Cleveland was President, Thomas Edison had just been awarded a patent for the telegraph, and The *Pledge of Allegiance* was first recited in public schools.

Their story is unique because they met totally by chance. Sarah was working as a food server for a boarding house (in Chicago) where Aaron resided. One evening after his meal, Aaron returned to the dining area to ask Sarah for a date. I don't have many details, but I can imagine that they quickly became a couple and went on to raise a large family. To be exact, they had eleven children! *Today, that would qualify them for a TV reality show*. I suppose back then, it was not entirely unusual. Grandpa Stein worked for Federal Huber that was headquartered in Chicago. In the 1920's, Federal Huber decided to move their plant to the old Cyrus McCormack Reaper Plant (its place of invention) in Plano, Illinois.

Just as the Plant moved, so did my grandparents. Off they went with all eleven children. My grandfather was a foreman with the Plant and thought that the move was necessary for the advancement of his career.

You can imagine how eleven kids from the city of Chicago must have impacted this very small farm town of 1,000 in Plano, Illinois! In turn, they must have felt quite a change from their own Chicago roots. The children were Abe, Fred, Max,

Great Grandfather

Aaron and Sarah Stein and Family

Aaron and Sarah Stein in 1946

**Lester, Molly & Ivan Newtson
Marion Knutson & Harry Stein**

Lillian, Mildred, Meyer, Jean, Freida, Katie, Bill, and my dad, Harry. The only things I know about them are that Max dove into the local swimming hole (a dammed up creek) and hit his head on a rock. He was never the same. Bill met and married Betty Mansfield, and Harry met and married Nettie Newtson (my mother). At this point, Sarah said she was going to move back to Chicago before any more of her children married "locals!" Grandpa Stein commuted back and forth on the train, but for most of the week he stayed home with us in Plano. This was all during the Depression when my dad was one of the lucky ones to have a job that paid $15 a week.

Grandma Sarah Stein was lauded to be an excellent cook. In fact, anyone who visited the Steins at their second-floor apartment was immediately asked to turn left into the kitchen to eat—no matter what time of the day. If not, she'd ask, "Excuse me, are you sick?" *She always had soup on the stove and big kosher pickles available!*

When we visited our grandparents, we always had a great time. They told wonderful stories to me about my dad when he was a kid. One that I remember is the story of how they all slept three in a bed (like logs) since there were so many kids and so little space. They also told me the story of how my dad left the house at the age of 16 and lied about his age to join the Marines in 1922. I loved to hear the tales of how he traveled all over the world on a Battleship. I always looked forward to seeing my grandparents. The adults would laugh, dance, and play poker while the country boys (Jerry and I) would wrestle with the two city boys (Buddy and Melvin). We were all about 13 years old at the time. *I wonder who won most of those wrestling matches.* For entertainment, my parents would go to Long's Barn, a farm in Kaneville, Illinois, for dancing. This activity was originally started as a barn-raising party. It was so much fun that farmer (Art Long) decided to turn it into a nightclub! Imagine a 100-foot bar that was originally designed to be a cattle station! (It was where the cattle stood while they were milked.) Long's Barn became a popular spot. People came from far and wide to dance to the latest bands!

2

The Newtsons

A Look Back at my Mother's Parents

Bert Osmond Newtson (1879-1963) married Maggie Caroline Peterson (1881-1921). They had seven children: Nettie (1901-1937—my mother), Gerald, Lester, Percy, Bernice, Ivan, and Mae (died just after birth). From birth records, it looks like they added a new baby every two years for 14 years. Maggie died at age 39, leaving my mother with the responsibility of looking after her younger siblings.

After Maggie's death, Grandpa Bert Newtson continued to farm in the Millbrook, Illinois area. The farm had a creek that flowed through part of it. The infamous Al Capone rented a farm building from Bert for the purpose of housing an illegal "still." I suppose it was an offer he couldn't refuse! His boys would unload the sugar and other necessary stuff from the trucks after dark. Then came the notice from the Feds: *Reward to anyone who turns in a person operating a "still."* Panic struck, and everything used for the production of this illegal liquor was immediately dumped into the creek. They thought that the evidence had been sufficiently hidden.

But soon thereafter, all the neighbors' cows and chickens were getting drunk from the creek water. This gave good reason to call the Feds. And in they came. Bert Newtson's farm was raided with sub-machine guns in hand. The "still" was totally busted up. Luckily, my Uncle Ivan escaped through the orchard and went to Joliet, Illinois where Bert was selling used cars. He told Bert about the big raid at the farm. Al Capone hired a lawyer for his man who was involved and another lawyer for Bert. *The legal papers kept Bert out of jail, but he nearly lost the farm.*

I spent one summer on the farm where I remember going out to get the cows for milking and rounding up the chickens for picking eggs. My cousin, Marion, would never help gather the eggs because the darned chickens attacked us (peck-

Mable & Bert Newtson
Home & Grocery store in Sandwich, IL

Maggie, Nettie, Gerald, Bert
Percy, Lester & Bernice Newtson

1915--Serine Ingemunson, Cyrus Munson, Hattie Hill, Clarence Larson, Deane Olson,
Elmer Helgeson, Victor Mortvedt, Millard Hanson, Gerhard Bjelland, Sidney
Anderson, Nora Anderson, Helena Fritz, Mabel Thorson, Nettie Newtson, Mildred Larson,
Addie Axland, Erving Likeness, Lyle Peterson, Clair Munson, Rev. A.O. Mortvedt,

**Lester Newtson Harold Stein
& Marion Knutson**

Hal with the Newtsons

Molly Washburn-Newtson Olson

11

ing) like someone had put batteries inside of them! One day, I came up with the ingenious idea of using a board to jack up the chickens while I picked the eggs so they wouldn't peck me. *It worked, but Marion almost died laughing.*

Another thing that interested me was the machine used to separate the cream from the milk (Separator). It worked through centrifugal force since the cream was heavier than the milk. Speaking of milk, I also learned to churn butter from milk as well as how to make ice cream. *It's a wonder I didn't go into the farming business!*

Grandpa Bert Newtson was a huge man—over six feet tall and 250 pounds. He was a "man's man," and from what I understand, in his younger years, was the county's best fighter. His hands were huge—big as a slab of meat—and he didn't mind fighting at the drop of a hat in his younger days. Those huge hands were good for lots of things. Now that I think of it, he used them to become the champion corn picker in Iowa.

Several years after Maggie died, Bert married Mable Payton Washburn, a piano player and entertainer at *The Tellings* in Plano. They married at Bert's home in Sandwich, Illinois, raised turkeys, and then turned part of their home into a grocery store. Years later, they moved to Big Rock, Illinois where Bert farmed the Love Farm.

Grandpa Newtson spent most of his life as a farmer, but in later years, he drove a gravel truck. He loved to play Pinochle, laugh, and have all kinds of fun. *Great guy, and proud to be a Norwegian!*

3

Christmas as a Kid

One Christmas Eve, we attended the Plano Lutheran Church. This was my very first church experience, and I remember attending every Sunday thereafter on my own (without any parent). Although I didn't have a parent with me, I chose to go with either a neighbor or another family member. Even then, church was an important part of my life. I remember getting up in front of the whole congregation to say my memorized Christmas piece (a Bible verse). I have to admit it—my knees were shaking! Sometimes I felt like I could barely stand. At the end of the service, everyone received a small box of candy. As soon as the service was over, my aunt and uncles (Newtsons) and my dad would drive to Newark to Aunt Tina and Uncle Oscar's farm for our big Christmas party. There were gifts for everyone and always the traditional fare—Oyster Stew! They had a player piano: *I loved to pump the pedals and play all the old favorites while everyone sang.*

My Early Years

I was born on December 9, 1931—just after midnight. Snow was up to the top of the fence posts.

Just for the record, 1931 must have been a tough year for everyone after the big Stock Market crash in 1929. Herbert Hoover was President. Unemployment had doubled, and many car manufacturers were going out of business. An average house cost $6,790 in 1931, and the average house rental was $18/month. Gasoline was 10 cents a gallon, a loaf of bread was 8 cents, and wages averaged $1,850.00 per year. *The most positive event of 1931 was the completion of The Empire State Building—the largest building in the world.*

My parents were Nettie (Newtson) a full-blooded Norwegian, and Harry Stein who was Latvian and Romanian. Harry was a non-practicing Jew and Nettie was a Lutheran. Harry was baptized as a Christian before he died. At that time, I asked the Pastor if it was okay to baptize him. Without hesitating, he said, "Yes," and so did my father. I had a very strong feeling that day that God was present.

My mother died when I was only six, so I have very few memories of her except what people in town told me about her. They said that many people loved my mother, and she was highly respected for her dedication to her siblings and her son (me). Her funeral produced the largest procession that Plano had ever seen.

After my mother died in 1937, my dad drove to California with his sister and her husband. I stayed in Plano with Dad's good friends, the Jack Parish family. My dad returned after three months, and we all moved in with another family who were also very good friends. Their names were Norm (Toomey) and Alma Burson. During this time from 1938-1943, Dad ate his meals across the street with other single men, while I ate with the Bursons. Mr. Burson worked in painting and wall papering houses, so in those days we made many baskets from his wallpaper samples. The idea was to make a large basket and fill it up with candy, drop it off at a favorite girlfriend's house, ring the doorbell, and run! The Bursons also loved to play golf, which served as my introduction to caddying. I made 50 cents a round, and if I ever made one dollar, I felt that I was flushed with cash.

Living with the Burson family was a wonderful experience for me. We rented a room from them, but they were above and beyond typical landlords. Mrs. Burson was a very loving person who treated me like her own child. She kept me under her wing from the ages 7-13 and really served as a surrogate mother for that time. Everyone in town really loved her. In fact, she was such a giving person, all the "Hobos" would come to her house for a free meal before they would get back on the train and ride to wherever. That was welfare in those days. Although we were poor, I never felt poor because of all the love I received. With little money to spend, we had to eat what was available: pheasant, rabbit, squirrel, and even pigeon pot pie. We also ate the frog legs that we caught in the pond. I was intrigued by the way the frogs still jumped as we cooked them in the frying pan.

The Bursons and their son, Norman Junior, trapped for skins. Sometimes I went with them to check the traps. We got muskrats, mink, otter, and an assortment of other wild animals. Mr. Burson then skinned the animals and dried them on boards to sell. *All this had become normal, everyday life for me.*

When I was quite young, I also watched Mrs. Burson's brother butcher a pig. Afterward, the men worked together to make sausage from the intestines and they ground up the pork with spices. They also deep fried the fat and made chitlins.

The six years that I lived with the Bursons were great since there were many kids in the neighborhood who were one or two years older than I. We had rubber gun contests (strips of sections of inner tubes stretched over a board with a clothes pin for a trigger), snowball fights, hockey events on a frozen pond, and as many games as our imaginations could ponder. In the summer, we would go swimming in a local creek. (I was thrown in, and it was "sink or swim.") We also played a lot of baseball in an empty lot between two houses. Since I was the only left-handed player, the others used to pitch to me "inside," and I invariably would put the ball through the Johnson's window. (Of course we would scatter, but it was no secret that I had hit the ball.) *Finally, the Johnsons got smart and put up chicken wire over their window.*

In addition to the time I spent with the Bursons, I visited often with my Aunt Bernice who was my mother's only sister. I later learned that (in her last days) my mother asked Aunt Bernice to look after me if she should pass away. So, in the summers, I visited Aunt Bernice in Chicago for as long as two weeks at a time. Bernice was a long-distance operator for the phone company, but she always found time to spend with me. The time we spent together was always very special. We went to Riverview Amusement Park and rode on all the amazing rides.

Donna Anderson, Hal Stein,
Nellie Ness, Ann Hendrickson,
June Schuning, Lois Schleslag,
and Pastor Alvin Johnson

Hal age six

MRS BURSON

We took the Milwaukee Clipper across Lake Michigan and had a lot of fun along the way. Once, my uncle teased me, so to pay him back, I tossed his bowler hat into the lake! *It sailed away!*

Bernice and LaVerne were both born on the same day (October 3, 1908) within hours of each other's farms. They were married at age 43, but they never had children. *That must be the reason that I was the apple of their eyes!* My only complaint about Aunt Bernice was that she had the bad habit of licking her handkerchief and using it to clean my ears! *I guess I can laugh about that today!*

Back in Plano, chasing after fires was a big social event. Fires really got our attention. Whenever a fire alarm sounded, we all rushed over to the Nelson's house because they had a cattle truck that could hold many people in the back end. We all jumped in and it was common to hear people say, *"Hi. I haven't seen you since the Wicks barn burned down."* Volunteer firemen in those days were excellent First Responders. At the sound of a fire alarm, the crew immediately rushed off to perform their heroics. Protocol was to climb onto the roof and use their hatchets to cut the biggest hole possible. *I remember a time when I watched this happen, only to learn that the fire was actually in the neighbor's backyard.*

In the winter, we had a place for sledding called *The Royal Bumps*. It was a very exciting place and, as the name implies, it was really bumpy!

They say, "It takes a village to raise a child." Well, that was certainly true in Plano. Everyone knew my dad, and they also knew that my mom had died. So … they all watched out for me. *I knew everyone in town.*

My twelfth year was a great one for me. I joined the Boy Scouts and that opened up all kinds of possibilities. We had a scout cabin about two miles from town that we hiked to for our Tuesday night meetings. Mrs. Jay, the scoutmaster's wife, made chili for us. I thought this was really living "large." We built huge bonfires, sang songs, and played "capture the flag." I also attended Boy Scout Camp that year where I learned to canoe, tell ghost stories, and do all kinds of other "scout" (secret) stuff. *At camp, I got the nickname that has lasted my whole life—Stoogy.* Most people in Plano did not call me by my real name. In fact, whenever my name was in the paper (sports and events), it was always *Stoogy. I don't think people even knew I had a real first name.*

When I was 13, I was confirmed in the Plano Lutheran Church where I always attended Sunday services. After two years of studying with the minister, I knew I was well prepared for this spiritual milestone. Again, it was time for the shaking knees from the excitement of being asked questions in front of the congregation. Happily, I passed with flying colors, and was officially a confirmed member of the church. I saved the photograph of the occasion. It's me with five girls. *Yes, I was the shortest in the group!*

I got my Social Security Card at age twelve because I was a pinsetter at the local bowling alley. My workers and I picked up pins and put them into a machine to set them on the alley for the next ball. I made $1.50 per night setting pins from 7 to 11 PM. *Although it was hard work, that was a lot of money to me.* For extra money, I also worked at the golf course during the summer months. I made $0.50 per round of 9 holes. On a good day, I could earn $1.50 for 27 holes. *In other words, I had to make my own spending money.*

At 13, I really had a good job. I worked at the Yorkville State Game Farm raising pheasants. I earned $135 per month doing this kind of farm work. I was responsible for a certain number of brooder houses (feed and water) as well as repairing fences, unloading feed (100-pound bags), and other chores. I also learned to drive at the Game Farm. I drove a big state truck with a 4-gear stick shift on the floor. Most of the guys working there were around my age because most of the older men were involved in the War (WWII) or were working in defense plants. This was quite a time with 13 and 14 year-old kids driving big trucks, often backing into brooder houses, and taking out sections of fences as they learned.

This was also a time of *rationing* (meat, canned goods, gas, etc.). Each family was given a coupon book to be used when buying these commodities. In the United States, nationwide food rationing was instituted beginning in the spring of 1942. Each and every member of a family (including babies) were issued a rationing book by the Office of Price Administration (OPA). These books contained stamps and gave precise details of the amounts of certain types of foods that you were allowed. Rationing insured that everyone could get a fair share of the items that were in short supply due to the war effort. Rationing didn't end until August of 1945. Sugar rationing continued until 1947. Citizens were asked to turn in old tires, raincoats, garden hoses, and rubber gloves. Americans were asked to cut back on their driving (to save rubber), to drive slower (to save gas), and to share rides. Gasoline was nationally rationed in December of 1942. If anyone wanted to make a major purchase such as a car, a bicycle, or a kitchen appliance, they had to obtain a special certificate to show proof of need. Americans were also asked to turn in scrap metal, and give fat from meat back to the butcher (for explosives). In 1943, every person had 48 points (in stamps) to be used for canned goods. I vividly remember the outcome of a cattle train wreck in Plano during these tough times *All the local butchers quickly arrived on the scene to make certain that Plano would have the luxury of good meat for some time.*

I was 13 the year that my dad married Leone Smith and we left the Bursons to live in her house. *What a place!* I had to sleep upstairs (no heat) and it had an outside toilet. Yes, *we really had to get up and go outside to the toilet. This was especially tough in winter!*

5

High School

I started high school at the age of 13. In fact, I was the youngest in my class. Plano High School had an unusual initiation of freshmen. If a freshman was caught by an upperclassman anywhere outside of school, they had the entitlement of taking our pants from us. Once my cousin (Jerry) and I went to a movie. When we walked out of the theater, there were some junior guys waiting for us. Of course, they took our pants, and we had to run through town "pant less" all the way to the cemetery to retrieve our duds. One time they took the pants of *all* the freshmen and tied them to the crossbar of the football goal posts. *You can imagine our trying to jump up to retrieve our togs while the whole school was watching through the school windows!*

Speaking of football, we were told by the school officials that if we wanted a football field, we would have to cut all the sod on the old field and move it to make room for construction. *We rolled up our sleeves and got busy.* My school had such a tight budget that no one on the freshmen team got a lettered jersey. I was so proud when, as a sophomore, I made the second team and got a numbered jersey even though it had a hole in it. (We were undefeated that year.) My position was defensive safety when we scrimmaged the first team. I had a unique way of tackling them and by using my arm, I could trip them instead of hitting those big guys head on. I would have gotten killed if I hadn't used this technique of tackling. It stopped them! *They were frustrated by a skinny 14 year-old and his tackling results!*

In my junior year, I made the first team as a left end (wide receiver). About the fifth game, I went up high for a pass and the defender came straight down on my foot. At the half, the doctor looked at it and said it was a bad sprain (not a break), so I played the rest of the game. After the game, I went to a party and tried to dance. My dancing just turned into lots of hobbling around. The next day it really hurt, so I decided to walk down to the doctor's office. I got about one block when my best friend, Dick Sauer, came by in his car and gave me a lift.

Hal in high school

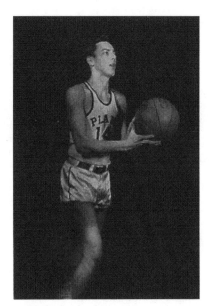

Hal in high school

X-Rays disclosed that three bones on my left foot were broken. *No more football that year.*

My senior year was a lot better. I was elected co-captain of the football team and played *wide receiver* on offense and *guard* on defense. That year, our first game was in Mazon, Illinois on a former oat field that had been cut but was still pretty rough. Early in the game, I got kicked in the mouth (no mouth guards then), lost two teeth, and chipped another in half. Later that game, I went on to catch a pass for a touchdown. *We won that one 6-0!*

In addition to playing wide receiver, I was the *kicker* for the team. Two games after losing my teeth, I followed my own kickoff down the field and tackled the receiver. I had a bad habit of putting my tongue between my teeth whenever I exerted energy, so as I made the tackle I bit my tongue. At halftime, they took me to the doctor's office where I had three stitches in my tongue (apparently so I wouldn't swallow it). It took three grown men to hold me down while the doctor stitched it up. *I was told that if I had bitten it any worse, I could have been tongue- tied.*

My high school basketball career was great—not because I was so good, but because I loved to play. I played *forward* and was considered to be the *spark plug.* This meant that I was the most aggressive player who also got the most fouls. We had a good team my senior year. *In fact, we won the conference (19 wins and 8 losses).*

I never realized how different the basketball was then versus now. As an example, we played one small school (even smaller than ours) and to make a long shot, you had to shoot through the rafters in the ceiling. Of course, our long shots through the rafters were only worth two points—it wasn't until 1986-87 that high schools even adopted the three-point rule. We traveled to our away games in the Plano school bus. It was a homemade contraption with a long body on a pickup chassis. The guys would infuriate the driver by clustering together in the back of the bus to tip it up. *No wonder there was a loss for drivers!*

I've also got to mention my four-year stint with high school Track & Field. Freshman year I ran track, hurdled, and did the 60-yard dash. Sophomore year I ran the mile. Junior year I focused on the 440, and senior year the 100-yard dash.

I also loved all the high school activities. I was in the Junior Class and Senior Class Plays. I served on the High School Student Council, and was President of my senior class. *That allowed me the honor of speaking at the graduation ceremony.*

Throughout high school, I stayed active in Explorer Scouts (Boy Scouts). The city let us recondition the second floor of an old city building for our headquarters. Windows were broken, pigeon poop was all over the place, and it was a real mess. We all pitched in and sanded the floors, installed new windows, and painted the place the best we could. We gave it the official name, *The Hang Out*. To pay for all the above improvements, we picked corn (left in the fields), hauled ashes (coal furnaces), and sold Christmas cards in the neighborhood. We totaled about $2,000 and with that, we renovated the building, bought a jukebox, a stereo, a pool table, a ping-pong table, and one of the first televisions in town. (It was a nine- inch black and white.) I was elected chairman of *The Hang Out* and worked closely alongside my idol, Glen Simms (the adult leader).

The kids chaperoned themselves in those times and never had a problem with drinking, smoking, or fighting. *Every Friday night, if we wanted to be open, we waxed the floors on hands and knees.* The *Hang Out* was so successful that it was written up in "*Boy's Life*" magazine.

When I was 15, I went on a two-week canoe trip with Senior Scouts. The trip started in Minocqua, Wisconsin and traveled 75 miles portaging from one lake to another. The journey to the site was a four-hour ride in the back of a pickup truck. *We were really up for anything in those days!* After paddling all day, we prepared the camp at night, dug latrines, set up tents, built fires for cooking, sang songs, and told ghost stories. One night, we grilled a porcupine and used the quills as toothpicks! As a scout, I was an Indian dancer. Our scoutmaster was really into Indian lore. We performed rain dances, eagle dances, and wolf dances—all dressed up in Indian garb.

In high school, no one had a car except for the farm kids. My friend, "Dopey" Daley, had an old car with very poor brakes, so when he dropped me off he would just slow down and I would jump out. *Good thing I was athletic!* Gasoline rationing was in effect during my high school years, so there was very little "joy riding." The only way to ride was to siphon gas out of cars that were parked in the alley behind the local bar. I do remember, in my junior year, a couple of older friends had a car and invited my best friend (Dick Saur) and me to see a Bear's game. In those days, it was held at Wrigley Field (a famous baseball park). Prior to the game, we stopped at Maxwell Street to see a series of little booths manned mostly by Jewish vendors. The only way that people could make purchases was to haggle for the best price possible. My prize purchase that day was a six-pack of argyle socks. I ended up getting them marked down to $1 from the original price of $5. When I got home, I saw that the socks were actually defective. *Although the haggling might be in my DNA, I'm not sure I got the best end of that deal.*

Anyway, the Bears game was really exciting with names like Bulldog Turner and Bronko Nagurski. I loved the whole experience of that game: the roar of the crowd, the smell of the vendors, and the taste of victory. *That day, I was officially hooked and have become a lifetime fan of the Chicago Bears.*

In May of every year, the music teacher put on a big "May Fete" extravaganza. Every class performed something special. In my senior year, the boys and girls danced the Maypole dance to music. It involved interweaving long, colored strands of cloth into beautiful designs. *Guys wouldn't be caught dead doing this today.*

My dad bought a house while I was in high school. The price was $3,500. It had an oil-stove for heating, and my room was derived from a former closet. *I remember that I could jump out of bed and hit the wall.* One day, my dad announced that he was going to put a basement under the house. Every night after dinner, we had to dig and shovel dirt onto a conveyer to be lifted into a wheel barrel to be hauled to the lot next door. One night, we were eating dinner and a heck of a racket could be heard from the basement. Although the house was up on jacks, the cement block had come tumbling down. *Not good.*

My dad sold that house, and we went on to build (I helped) a house next door. Even though we both worked hard on the house, this one ended up costing $16,000. My room was actually the unfinished upstairs. In the winter, it was very cold up there. (The only little bit of heat was that which was generated from the lower level.) Conversely, when summer came around, it was very hot up there. *Maybe that's the reason that extreme temperatures don't bother me.*

At the age of 15, I got a job working at a plumbing factory. It wasn't just any plumbing factory—it was the one where my grandfather, dad, and uncle also worked. *It was special because I ended up working there all the way through high school and college.* My first job was in the Core Room part of the Foundry. The temperatures reached up to 130 degrees in the summer with lots of smoke. My job was to bend the wires that gave the cores stability. The molten brass would be poured into molds and it would form around the sand cores to form a faucet. I started at 55 cents an hour, and by the time I left, I was making $1.35. I worked in every department including shipping, chrome plating, and running a tourit lathe that drilled and put thread on faucets. *Although this was a very boring job, I was able to work 60+ hours a week and 20 of those hours were time-and-a-half.* I ended up making $1,500 in the summer. Supplemented by work during Christmas and spring vacations, I had enough to pay for college, clothes, and a little spending money. Most of the spending money actually came from the many jobs I had in college.

6

College Years

College was a wonderful experience for me. I chose Dubuque University for several reasons. First, the Plano School Superintendent had taken me under his wing so to speak and advised that Dubuque would be a good match for my needs. It was highly academic, and it was a school that offered a good student/work program. I had limited funds, and he knew that paying my own way was an important factor. *No one from my mother or dad's family had ever gone to college.* It seems amazing to think about, but I had never seen Dubuque University until the day I arrived for my freshman year. My dad didn't even know where it was located. In fact, he almost dropped me off at the wrong place—Loras College—a Catholic College in town (Dubuque).

Dubuque was a small Presbyterian college with about 1,000 students. Although it was considerably small (large to me), it had students from all over the world because of their affiliation with the church. This was great for me because I now had friends who were Asian, African American, farmers, city kids from NYC, and a mix of others from Chicago. *We were all one, big, happy family.*

My college experience gave me the chance to grow in many areas. I took part in college plays (Sir Walter Raleigh in *Elizabeth the Queen*), I was involved in Student Government, and I was a member of a fraternity. I also worked and managed to maintain good grades. My college jobs were quite simple: washing pots and pans in the kitchen, waiting on tables, and working odd jobs for a local doctor. I also started my own cleaning business with my roommate, Paul DeBeer. Students dropped off cleaning at our room, and we sent it off to a local cleaner. We advertised in the school paper: ***DeBeer Stein Cleaners.*** *What a great name!*

Student Government was a lot of fun. I was on the Student Council, and in my senior year I was elected President of the Student Body. We had a big election campaign, a campaign manager, and election posters all over the campus. "***You can't oppose the man with the nose!***" *I still remember the speech I gave about my* *platform*. After I won the election, my work as President of the Student Body required a weekly speech at school assemblies and then at college graduation. My work as President took away from the time I needed to spend on jobs, so Dubuque gave me a $380 activities' scholarship for which I will always be indebted. *To this day, I continue to give back.*

My Dubuque fraternity was *Phi Omicron*. We called it *Phi O*, and it was noted as the best on campus. We had all the campus leaders, but most importantly, the best parties! The President of Phi Omicron was the captain of the Dubuque basketball team. He was African American and one of the most respected guys on campus. Fraternity initiation was tough back then. We had to carry little notebooks around our necks for members to write notations. They sounded like this: *"He didn't shine my shoes the way I like them shined. He didn't run as fast as I told him to. He didn't answer me when I spoke to him."* Then unfortunately, we met every night to pay for our sins by receiving a major paddling on our butts. *I still have my paddle.* The final night of *Hell Week*, we were tarred and feathered with molasses and corn flakes. We were ordered to lie on the floor while the "actives" climbed up on a ladder to drop raw eggs into our open mouths. After many other all-night indignities, we finally went out together for breakfast. *In some sick way, this bonded us together as fraternity brothers.*

College summers were also a lot of fun for me. Although I worked six days a week, I still went out every night with my friends. Sundays were the most fun because three of us would joy ride in Wally Malmborg's *Model T* convertible. John Peterson played the ukulele and the three of us drank beer and sang to our hearts' content. We usually ended up at the Sheridan swimming hole (a former gravel pit) where we would pick up girls to go to a movie.

One Sunday it rained, so Dick Sauer who had a 1939 Chevy sedan joined us. We decided that since there were now four of us, we needed to buy more beer. All four of us joined in the storytelling, singing, and drinking. About one mile out of town, Dick's car got a flat tire and we found ourselves in a bind. Try as we did, the tire would not come off of the axle. John decided to run into town for help, and the rest of us just followed along behind him. When we arrived at the Snack Shop (kids' hang out), we were all soaking wet, and with all the beer sloshing around in my stomach—I was sick. I rushed straight into the toilet with Wally hot on my heels. Needless to say, I lost my cookies, and as soon as I did, Wally flushed the toilet. Disaster! I said, *"Jeez, Wally, you just flushed my teeth down the john!"* When we came out of the bathroom, all the kids were laughing hysterically. I knew it would be tough to explain things when I got home. I told my dad I must have eaten something that disagreed with me. He said, *"You really shouldn't eat at that greasy spoon place!"* Just about everybody in town heard about this incident, and in fact, the local dentist made me a new partial plate for $35 since he knew I was working my way through college. *That was another act of kindness toward me.*

Stein Is Voted Top Student Leader-'52-'53

Harold Stein

Harold Stein, of Plano, Ill., and of junior status at the University of Dubuque, was elected on April 25, to the presidency of the Student Senate for the school year of 1952-53.

Continuing his leadership in student affairs from high school, Harry has taken an active part in student affairs at Dubuque University by being a member of the Student Council for two years, Phi Omicron Fraternity for three years, and the theater board for one year.

During the two years as a council member, Harry's main accomplishments were v i c e president, chairman of the student union committee and atten- dance at the state conference of the National Student Association.

Vigorously campaigning from April 23-24, with the help of pro Stein students, Harry completed his campaign with a speech before the whole student body on the 25th of April. In this speech Harry presented his ideas for a more progressive Student Senate. **His platform is as follows:**

1. Suggestion Box.

2. Affiliation with the National Student Association.

3. Standing Committees for special student projects.

4. Monthly Assemblies of student body.

5. Co-operations of classes and senate.

6. Co-operation of administration and senate.

7. More student activities to interest everyone.

8. Student organized orientation program for freshmen.

9. Continue to strive for a student union.

There were two other junior candidates on the final ballot. T h e y were **Don Swain** of St. Louis, Mo., and **Maurene Julius** from Morland, Ia. These two, along with Stein had previously been selected in a primary ballot which covered all petitions which were filed.

Take a Cue From Coppage

This issue of the **CUE** is largely the work of George Coppage, associate editor. George has applied for the editorship for next year.

College Graduation - Commencement speaker

College Graduation - Leading the procession

Who's Who Among Students
IN AMERICAN UNIVERSITIES AND COLLEGES

THIS PUBLICATION IS NOT THAT OF A. N. MARQUIS & CO. OR THE PUBLICATION KNOWN AS "WHO'S WHO IN AMERICA"

H. PETTUS RANDALL
EDITOR

P. O. BOX 934
Tuscaloosa, Alabama

October 31, 1952

Mr. Harold Gene Stein
223 Steffens Hall, University of Dubuque
Dubuque, Iowa

Dear Mr. Stein:

You were recommended to us recently for recognition in the 1952-53 Edition of WHO'S WHO AMONG STUDENTS IN AMERICAN UNIVERSITIES & COLLEGES. It is a pleasure to tell you that your nomination has been accepted.

The students recognized in WHO'S WHO AMONG STUDENTS IN AMERICAN UNIVERSITIES & COLLEGES each year are nominated from approximately 650 colleges and universities. Campus nominating committees are instructed, in making their selections, to consider the student's scholarship; his cooperation and leadership in academic and extracurricular activities; his citizenship and service to the school; his promise of future usefulness.

WHO'S WHO AMONG STUDENTS IN AMERICAN UNIVERSITIES & COLLEGES awards each member a certificate of recognition, presented on the campus either at graduation or earlier in the year. An adjunct to our international honor program is the placement service, conducted for the benefit of seniors and graduates. There is no cost to the student for inclusion in the publication or for any services rendered by the organization.

Before you fill in the blank forms that accompany this letter, please read the Instruction Sheet; this sheet explains the nature of each form and the purpose for which it will be used. It is your responsibility to complete your forms carefully, particularly the two Biography Blanks and to mail your completed forms to this office promptly. So there will be no chance of omission, we recommend that your forms be returned within ten days.

Our staff wishes to add its compliments to those you have received on the campus and to extend you a cordial welcome. We hope you will consider this recognition a small reward for work well done and an encouragement for the future.

Sincerely yours,

H. Pettus Randall
Editor

ms
Enc.

Don Swinniker and I bought a 1929 Chevy near the end of my junior year. The deal was I would have the car the first half of the summer, and he would have it the last half. It really wasn't much of a car since we only paid $30 for it and the insurance was $45 for six months. The car didn't have very good brakes, either. *When I drove it through the steep hills of Dubuque, the only way I could slow down was to pull on the emergency brake.* To put it mildly, the drive from Dubuque to Plano was exciting. I made it as far as Sandwich, Illinois (five miles from Plano) when I stopped to show my car to Frankie Mall. Frank had a new Buick, and he volunteered to trade cars for the trip to Plano. I was so used to pushing a brake to the floor that when I just tapped on Frankie's Buick brakes, I was almost thrown through the window!

By the way, Frankie Mall and his wife Peg were the best friends of Aunt Bernice (my mom's sister). Frankie was one of my biggest supporters when I played basketball. Everyone could hear him yelling at me, *"Come on, Punkie!"* Punkie was his nickname for me.

In college, I had a variety of friends from all different walks of life. There were athletes, religious people, foreigners, geeks, drinkers, nurses, and even professors. My advisor was Reuben Austin (Kim and Chris had him too) who sometimes came up to my room to discuss interesting issues. My major was Economics with a minor in Psychology. Even though Professor Austin and I disagreed on many topics, I still received excellent grades from him. The grades paid off because in my senior year I was selected to be in *"Who's Who in American Colleges and Universities."*

Graduation was great. I led the procession of faculty and students because I was the Student Body President. I also spoke at the Commencement. *It was an honor that I will always remember.*

7

Off To The Navy

After college graduation, Don Swain and I left for the Navy in Newport, Rhode Island. We kissed our girlfriends goodbye and boarded a train for our first stop—New York City. Since Don and I had several days before we had to report for duty, we decided to indulge in some Broadway shows and eat at some well-known restaurants. I attended Supply School in Newport for 16 weeks. Supply School was like a business school for the Navy. The school was structured for the selection of a man's location of assignment to be based on his class rank. *Since I was ranked second, I was able to get my first choice. It was Washington, D.C.*

Although I never experienced actual Sea Duty, I certainly had a great time in D.C. My job was in accounting for the Naval Receiving Station in Anacostia, Maryland. I completed the financial records for our base. *All in all, I must admit that it was not a high-stress position.* The mess hall in D.C. was something like I had never seen. We ate chipped lamb on toast, lamb patties, lamb chops, and then chipped lamb again for breakfast. I heard someone say that the Navy had a 60-year supply of canned lamb. *To this day, it's not exactly my favorite.*

During my time in Washington, D.C., I joined a Methodist church group of young singles. We had a ball: camping, concerts, dances, and more. At that time, there were ten single girls to every single guy, so I guess I had good pickins'. One of the girls I met worked for a senator, so I asked her if she could somehow get me into the Senate Gallery. The Senate was in the process of censuring Joe McCarthy (WI) for his drive to blackball suspected communists. Years later, I looked at the card she gave me to get in and was stunned to see that it was signed by Lyndon B. Johnson.

Navy bound

Summer Flashback

Speaking of politics, one summer when I was home from my junior year in college, my dad and I went to a double-header White Sox baseball game. This happened to be at the time that the Democrats were having their convention at the Stock Yard's Amphitheater. Between games, I told my dad that I wanted to go to the ballpark lobby to find out the name of the Democratic nominee for President. When I got there, someone told me that the headquarters was only two blocks away. So, I left the ballpark to find the International Amphitheater, which turned out to be 12 blocks away. I took a streetcar there to check things out. Once I got there, I found large groups of people standing outside who made their way into the building by holding up an envelope with a small white card inside. I found a white envelope that had fallen on the ground, picked it up, and put a fake card inside of it. I then showed my envelope and barged right into the main floor to the State of Washington Caucus.

I took full advantage of the situation by collecting all kinds of memorabilia. I got a banner and a coonskin cap, among other things. (I still have them.) And there on the podium was President Harry Truman introducing Adlai Stevenson, the Presidential Candidate. This was the second political convention to be televised coast-to-coast (following the Republican Convention weeks earlier). *I was ecstatic to be the young kid from Plano on the floor with all these big wigs.*

Since quite a bit of time had passed, I thought I'd better get back to my dad and the baseball game. Of course my dad immediately said, *"Where have you been?"* I showed him all the campaign items and he was shocked, to say the least. The year was 1952 (July), and Stevenson became the Democratic nominee. Stevenson went on to lose the election to President Eisenhower on November 4, 1952.

9

More Navy Memories

To get back to the Navy, we were given a 30-day leave every year. I took mine around Christmas of 1954. I hitchhiked from D.C. to Chicago, which was not an unusual thing to do in those days. From Chicago, I caught the train to Plano. Much to my surprise, my Uncle Bill was also on the train! Uncle Bill was the Superintendent of Federal Huber, the plumbing fixture company where my dad, grandfather, and cousin worked. Bill was on the train returning from Company headquarters where he had picked up the Christmas bonuses for the factory employees. He was actually carrying a *shoebox* with $34,000 cash in it! *At six feet two inches and 260 pounds, I would hope that no one would mess with him.*

Back at the Navy assignment—I was chosen to represent the Navy to work for the Secretary of Defense at the Pentagon for a program entitled *Defense Orientation Program.* It was designed to familiarize civilian business leaders with military activities. Actually, there were leaders from all walks of life. I remember Father Hesburg, the head of Notre Dame. I also remember meeting the CEO of both Ford and General Motors. My job was to facilitate tours and literature for these prominent individuals.

10

Honorably Discharged

I was honorably discharged from the Navy in 1955, and I had a job waiting for me as a Management Trainee for Sears ($65/week) in Aurora, Illinois. Just for the record, the minimum hourly wage in 1955 was $1 an hour, rent for a home was $87 a month, and a gallon of gasoline was 23 cents. McDonalds opened in 1955—*fast food was here!*

My training at Sears was to include work participation in every department of the store. The goal was to eventually become a store manager. After one year, I became very bored with the job, so I took the liberty of listing my name with an employment agency in Chicago. The agency got me an interview with Union Carbide in Chicago. The interview with Jack Van Winkle went very well. He said that all the top management from New York would arrive that day for a sale's meeting. He then told me that they would meet with me to decide if I were to be hired. If so, I would be invited to stay for their meeting. If not, I would be asked to go home. *They hired me!* My salary was set at $400 per month, and I was temporarily assigned to the Chicago office.

That night, after the meeting, all the guys sat down to play poker. A few of the top managers reached out to me and invited me to join in the game. I only had $10 in my pocket, but I boldly said, *"Yes."* I was unconsciously lucky that night and won about $70. The guys from New York kidded my new boss, *"You just hired a ringer who already beat us at poker!"*

I located a place to live in Chicago at 1300 N Astor. It was a big old brownstone building that had 12 guys living in it with an elderly landlady. We had a ball there since we were only one block from Rush Street (night clubs and bars). *This was the "in" place in Chicago at the time.*

After six months of training, I was assigned to Detroit, Michigan to call on service stations that sold Prestone Antifreeze. This was quite a chore since it was a time when all the discount stores were starting up. They were selling Prestone Antifreeze for $0.99 retail while the service stations were selling it for $3.25. *I learned how to get thrown out gracefully.*

My next assignment was to join a special crew to cover the territory of North Dakota and Northern Minnesota. The crew consisted of a technician and a salesman (me). We went into small towns where I invited all the service station employees to attend one of our demonstrations. We had three crews covering the area, and every weekend we met in Minneapolis for some fun. Some of these experiences were unbelievable. We went to a fireman's ball in Zap, North Dakota; had a first experience at a rodeo in Minot, North Dakota; and would you believe, actually spent time on an Indian Reservation. *All of this fun added up to great lifetime experiences!*

Eventually I was promoted to District Manager and was moved to the state of Indiana. My home base was Indianapolis. This is where I met my life-long friend, Carl Dilsaver. Carl preceded me in Indiana and kindly introduced me to all of the customers. Carl also introduced me to a guy named Al Carlson. Al asked me if I would be interested in buying a house with him. We also asked Dan Welsh and Ben Noll to join us in living there. The house was on 2 ½ acres of land, had 3 bedrooms, and a "great room" for entertainment. We paid $35,000 for it, and by each putting in $75 a month, Al and I could make our mortgage payment and have enough left over for food expenses. Drinks, of course, were separate. It was a beautiful place in the best part of town. The four of us decided that we needed an in-ground swimming pool, so I bought a special liner from Union Carbide. All we needed was a block foundation—so we went ahead and built it ourselves. We had some fabulous parties in that house with as many as 100 singles attending. In fact, we were twice written up in the Indianapolis newspapers. *"College Athletes' Bachelor Pad."* To this day, I don't know where the reporter came up with information that we were athletes. *Maybe it's because we served her several martinis!*

11

A Meeting of Good Fortune

Those parties led me to my first meeting with a girl named Lola. We were planning yet another party, so we stopped by our friend, Max Miller's place to invite him. Max's roommate, Don, told us that Max was with two girls who had invited him out to dinner. The two girls were Lola Stegner and Jean Hummermier who were among about eight or ten other people. *I didn't count them all, since I only had eyes for Lola.*

Well, we invited everyone to our party, but I especially made a point of inviting Lola. On the night of the party, we had a huge crowd of friends—*but no Lola.* The next day I called her. *"Lola, we missed you at the party. Why didn't you come over?"* Her answer was pretty clear. *"Well, you never came by to pick me up!"* I sure learned that lesson. *So much for general invitations!*

I did ask Lola for an official date to go to the Indianapolis 500 Race. We went in a large group and one of the guys was in charge of bringing the drinks. On the day of the race, the temperature was in the 90's. So, the heat plus the martinis brought as the only beverage, ended up creating a few headaches. My first date with Lola lasted from 8 AM until 12 PM, which included the race and all the after-parties. Lola's brother, Doug, who also lived with his family in Indianapolis, had a few things to say about me. Apparently he thought I must have been some kind of "Alky" to serve martinis to his sister at the Indianapolis 500!

That first date with Lola was May 30, 1958. We saw each other every day after that until the day we were married—November 15—of the same year. I remember proposing to Lola at Westlake in Indianapolis while the band played our song—*Tenderly*. I bought her diamond from a wholesaler in Chicago (Carl's friend). It was a one + carat emerald cut and was mounted in platinum with diamond baguettes.

I distinctly remember the day Lola and I flew from Indianapolis to Madison to share our engagement news with her parents. This was the first time for me to meet them. We arrived at the airport in plenty of time (or so we thought) and decided to have a coke in the airport café. We were so excited and engrossed in our conversation that we missed the plane. Her parents waited on the other end (Madison) and had to meet every arriving plane until we showed up.

12

Our Marriage

Lola and I were married in Madison, Wisconsin at the Lutheran Memorial Church on the campus of The University of Wisconsin on November 15, 1958. Lola and her mother (Stella) loved to shop, so they had a ball picking out her wedding dress and trousseau. They also selected china, silverware, and crystal. (Kim still has it.)

Our reception was held at the West Side Businessmen's Club in Madison. Jean Hummermier was her maid of honor and Carl Dilsaver was my best man. Many of our friends from Indianapolis joined us for the wedding. Our original plan was to fly out of Madison to our honeymoon, but we heard that my roommates were planning some sort of trick. Considering this, we decided to drive with Carl and his wife to Chicago and catch a plane the next morning. As we drove to Chicago, we decided to stop for a bite to eat. We walked into a restaurant and of all people— there was Grandpa Newtson along with Lee and Lester. *They got a big kick out of seeing us, but we were kind of out of it by that time.*

We spent our first night as a married couple at the Palmer House in Chicago. The next day we caught a plane for Nassau in the Bahamas. Nassau was a perfect honeymoon spot. The Island was so fun because we rented bicycles and rode all over the place. We went to Paradise Island before it was a gambling casino! We rented a boat and went out to see another Island. Our guide said we could buy it for only $15,000. *Today it's probably $15 million!* The people there were friendly and everyone seemed to be in a holiday spirit. We decided to buy straw bags for everyone in our families for Christmas. *I had fun haggling with the natives.*

When we got back to the Stegners, we had received so many wedding presents that we actually needed to rent a U-Haul. Part of the reason for the abundance of gifts was due to W.D. (Wesley DeWitt) Stegner who was a State Farm manager for the state of Wisconsin. It seemed that every agent sent along a present for us, including seventeen salad bowls! All of my Stein relatives gave us money that was easier to haul!

Our wedding

Ted Dewite, Lola, me, Burt Newtson

13

Lola and her Family

Lola Stegner grew up in Madison, Wisconsin. She was a graduate of the University of Wisconsin Business School and was an outgoing, friendly person. Lola definitely had an eye for style and had very good taste in clothing—in fact, Lola was a buyer for L.S. Ayres Department Store in Indianapolis when I met her.

By the way, Lola's father, *Steg,* was a very interesting character. He began his work at State Farm Insurance Company with its founder, a man named Meherle, who in fact wrote a book about starting State Farm. It was entitled, *The Farmer from Merna* (a small town outside of Bloomington, Illinois). *Lola used to laugh about the fact that, as a little girl, she used to bounce on Meherle's knee.* Steg was a very disciplined man who walked seven miles every day—even if it was winter. In this case, he walked around the furnace as many times as it took to complete his seven miles. *When we visited, I walked with him.*

Lola's mother, Stella, was just about the best mother-in-law a guy could ask for. We visited the Stegners every holiday, and Stella never failed to cook all my favorites. She was a fantastic cook. She and Steg played the organ, although Steg normally took over the keyboard after dinner. He played by ear and could play almost any requested tune. After his concerts, he always wanted to play cards. We played Cribbage, Old Maid, Gin, and Kings on the Corners. Steg was an excellent Cribbage player, but I was luckier than he was which drove him nuts. *If I didn't have the luck on my side, I'd never have won a game from him.*

The Stegner house was always a joyous place. When Lola and I had children, their toys would pile up high at the Stegners. We carted all the kids' gifts to Madison, and every Christmas Eve I assembled them into the wee hours of the night. I remember assembling a train track on a large piece of plywood in their kitchen and then realized that I couldn't get it into the living room. *So … I had to disassemble it and start all over again.*

Lola's parent's house

Lola's parents (Stella and Steg)

Everybody loved the Stegner's screen porch in the summertime. It had a nice hammock that the kids like to swing on. Once little Chris was swinging on it with Doug underneath. He just pushed it with his feet, and Chris went flying into the screen.

Steg loved golf and he played every day possible. He approached the green with a 5 wood, and with a big slice he could put that ball right on the green. He also liked to use his "*foot mashie*" on the green before he chomped on his cigar. "*Foot mashie" meant that he would move the ball with his foot.*

I distinctly remember Steg taking the whole family out to dinner at the A & W Root Beer restaurant where we always ordered the Moma Burgers. *Those were happy days for the whole family.*

14

First Home in Indianapolis

When we were first married, Lola and I lived in an apartment in Indianapolis. We did not have a laundry nearby, so Lola had to visit the "bachelor" house to wash clothes (the house I still owned with Al Carlson). It seems hard to believe, but our first child, Kim, was born 9 ½ months after we were married. Lola was in delivery for 27 hours but it was well worth the wait. We were so proud of our little girl. The 27 hours actually included the usual rush to the hospital (Methodist) only to be told to go home and come back when the contractions were closer.

We built our first house in Indianapolis for $24,000 and we thought it was a castle. It was all stone and had a lot of space. It had both a well and a septic system. Whenever it rained, the toilet would rise to the top. In fact, this happened to Stella once and from then on, if she had to go, we agreed to take her over to the shopping center. The well water also had fine grains of sand inside it that we didn't notice until one time when my folks were visiting. They noticed that there was sand in the bottom of their ice cubes. *In spite of these problems, we loved the place.*

My Bachelor house in Indianapolis

Our first home in Indianapolis

15

Finding Naperville

In 1963, I was promoted to District Manager in Chicago. Lola and I had only one week to find a home in the Chicago area. We spent most of the week looking in the Arlington Heights area since most of the guys from Union Carbide lived there. But—it was to no avail. On our way home to Plano to visit my folks, we decided to stop in Naperville, Illinois where there was a new subdivision being built (Maplebrook). *It was love at first sight.*

We talked to two builders and decided to hire a man named Don Tosi. We chose to build a Georgian Colonial with four pillars in the front. We paid $30,000 for the house. This house turned out to be fantastic—mostly because of the neighbors. There were the Brandlunds, LaRues, Pflumes, Schlankers, and others. We had more fun with these people. We got together, planned parties, and laughed so hard we would almost cry. We took dance lessons together, had picnics, went to parades (kids with bikes), attended birthday parties, and planted shrubs—*all with a lot of laughs!* Naperville was just a great town. I remember parade days when half the town was in the parade and the other half was watching it.

Indian Guides was very popular in Naperville. Kim, Doug, and Chris were all involved in it—each for three years. We were *Little Cloud and Big Thunder, Big Bow and Little Arrow, and Big Rock and Little Stone.* I remember camping outings. I also recall making vests to wear and totem poles to carry in the Memorial Day Parade. Everything was going well in Naperville and as I said, we really loved it there.

Lola and I joined Our Savior's Lutheran Church this year and really enjoyed it. We encouraged our children to participate in youth activities and Bible studies as well. All three of our children were eventually confirmed in this church, which gave us all a strong sense of pride.

Indian Princesses

16

Corporate Gypsies

Then, one night I got a call from my boss. *"Hal, congratulations. You've been promoted to Division Manager of the south to be headquartered in Memphis."* My new responsibility was to be the sales manager of all of Louisiana, Arkansas, Tennessee, Mississippi, Alabama, Georgia, and part of Florida. I would have a branch of salesmen in each of the major cities of these states. Lola and I felt like *Corporate Gypsies* at this point. We picked up our family and moved to Memphis, Tennessee—even though we hated to leave Naperville. After a week of looking at houses, Lola and I made the decision to build one in Germantown, a suburb of Memphis. The home we decided to build was actually more beautiful than anything I ever dreamed I could own. It was a Georgian Colonial with four large pillars (I could hardly reach my arms around them). The entire house was brick and was constructed on a three-level lot surrounded by trees. It had an intercom, an exposed aggregate driveway, a lighted walkway—the whole works—for only $40,000.

My new office in Memphis was on the 19th floor of a bank building overlooking the famous Peabody Hotel and the Mississippi River. *Imagine Hal "Stoogy" Stein with his own personal secretary!* We also had some very nice neighbors. I remember the Medlins, Gastaways, and others. It didn't take us very long to become acclimated to the southern culture. Well—now that I've said that—there *were* a few exceptions.

We had a lovely maid named Hattie who was like a part of our family. Our neighbors couldn't understand how we paid her a total of $7.50 a day while they only were paying $6.50. And according to others, sin of all sins, we enjoyed eating our meals together. *At that time in the south, Black people were seen in a different light.* Memphis was not integrated at that time. At the local nightclubs, I read signs that said to pay $1.00 to join and that you must carry your own bottle (a dry state). The $1.00 was to "Keep them colored out." *Lola and I had a hard time with that rule.*

Our New Jersey home

Our Memphis Home

Fishing with Kim and Doug in Wisconsin

47

I remember the night I flew in from a trip to Shreveport, Louisiana. It was April 4, 1968. When I landed, I was told that Martin Luther King had been assassinated in Memphis. (He was supporting a garbage hauler's strike at the time.) I was told that I might get stopped on my drive home—the entire town was totally up tight. When I finally did get home, Lola told me that our maid, Hattie, was going to sit up all night at her house with a shot gun on her lap. Hattie was worried that mobs might try to burn it down. *This single shot fired by James Earl Ray at Martin Luther King, Jr. sparked a wave of rioting in the black communities (not only in Memphis) of several cities around the United States.*

The schools in Memphis, Tennessee were quite shocking compared to those in Naperville, Illinois. Lola went to the kids' new school to register them, and the first man she met she though to be the janitor. *"Excuse, me, but I am here to meet the principal."* To her surprise, he said, *"I am the principal."* Things only went downhill from there. He told her that pre-registration was not necessary. He also told her that the school only hires substitute teachers, they put 40 children in each class, and that they only hire certified teachers *after* all this has been sorted out. Memphis did not even have a public kindergarten, so Doug went to a Baptist Church Pre-School. *The only thing he learned there was how to serve tea.*

I must admit that I really loved traveling in the south. The food was great (I learned to eat raw oysters), the people I worked with were great, and life was generally just fine. We were there (Memphis) for a total of two years.

17

Moving East

Then that famous phone call came. *"Hal, you've just been promoted to our largest division in the East Coast."* My new area of responsibility included New York, New Jersey, Pennsylvania, Virginia, Maryland, and Washington D.C. The main headquarters were in Cherry Hill, New Jersey. *Talk about culture shock! That was the end of hearing "Y'all come over, hear?"* I had to adapt a whole new mindset. *Everyone in the East was all business.*

We settled in and had been in New Jersey for about one year when I had a routine company physical examination. In the exam, the doctor discovered a mysterious spot of my lung. This was quite a surprise to hear since I had never smoked. The doctor said, *"We'll keep you under observation for six weeks, and if it gets larger, we will have to operate. If it is cancerous, there will be a 70% chance that you won't survive."*

During the six-week waiting time, we all took a trip to Niagara Falls. I think it was partially to get my mind off my medical issues, but it just turned out to be a scary time as it loomed over my head. The Falls were beautiful that time of the year (winter) with frozen areas and water flowing over and under the ice, but it was difficult to relax.

At the end of the six weeks of torment, new X-Rays were taken. Of the three radiologists readings, two believed that the spot had not changed but one thought it had grown slightly larger. My doctor referred me to a surgeon who advised me to undergo exploratory surgery. *Exploratory* sounds innocent, but it really isn't. That doctor cut through two of my ribs and opened me up like a can of sardines. When all was said and done, he only found a spot of tuberculosis that was encapsulated in calcium. The surgery was totally unnecessary and it almost killed me. I remember watching cockroaches crawling around the hospital room while I waited four days to find out if my spot was cancerous. *That doctor's bedside manner left a lot to be desired, too.*

18

Return to Naperville

Lola and I were rethinking a lot of things at this point in our lives. We decided that the East Coast life plus an accumulation of all the moves with Union Carbide (7 times in 13 years) was just too much. *We wanted to go back to Naperville and the life we had so enjoyed there.*

We knew a man named Hascal Hooper in Memphis who owned the local employment agency (Snelling and Snelling). I had hired people from Snelling and Snelling when I worked in Memphis, so I knew of Hascal's success. Lola and I ventured out and decided to start our own business. We went to Snelling and Snelling Owner's School for two weeks and then opened our own agency in Aurora, Illinois. Everything was possible because of the savings we had accrued. *Imagine that. We moved our whole family back to a new house in Naperville with only the promise of a new business.*

Lola was the original receptionist for the new business until we finally hired someone to take over. We also hired four counselors. Funny, but one of the counselors (Perle) said she could go to work if we would take over her dog, Sam. The employment agency was basically limping along when one night Lola and I went to a party and met up with Joe Rovin (my cousin's husband). Joe told me that he owned a plastics company (Chicago Transparent) and wanted to get into the Consumer Market. His dream was to compete with Union Carbide (Glad Bags) and Mobile (Hefty Bags) that were the advertised brands of bags. I gave Joe my best advice about what he could do to compete with these two mega companies. *Joe listened intently and then said, "Hal, if you can make this happen, I will pay you handsomely."*

I decided that this was an offer too good to pass up. I sold the employment agency to one of the counselors I had hired (Mike Shields) after only twelve months of being in business. Joe's plastic company was located in Chicago. I drove there, because it was on the north side. I began with some very successful sales with

Sears, Montgomery Ward, K-Mart, Osco, and many others. Joe Rovin was a great guy to work with, but his partner (Irv) was as bad as Joe was good. They never came through with the bonuses they had promised. After I had been there for about 18 months, a rep (Dick Means) invited me to lunch to discuss an idea. His brainstorm was to leave Chicago Transparent to start a whole new company. He had a few friends who were also interested in joining (John Schneiter and John Sellers). They were already producing plastic bags for the dairy industry and could convert some of their equipment to make more of them.

Woods of Bailey Hobson

My dad & I gambled on the Riverboat

19

Off to the Races

We decided to start a new company. I wanted to make the name sound important, so I came up with one that sounded rather global—North American Plastics. *I thought we would grow into the name.* Basically, John and Jack continued to run the dairy bag industry (Exact Packaging). I ran North American Plastics (NAP). To say we were undercapitalized is to put it mildly. We would ship during the week and then go to the bank on Fridays to borrow against our receivables. Sales started off with a bang; mostly because I knew all the buyers. We sold Osco, Sears, Montgomery Ward, Marshall Fields, Ace Hardware in Chicago, and to customers throughout the United States. I hired manufacture's reps in every market.

So, on we struggled for the next two years to keep our heads above the competition. At the two-year mark, two of my partners decided to sell their shares of the company. Of the three suitors who wanted to buy them out, I chose Harry Engh. Harry had formerly owned (actually his father owned) a company in Sycamore, Illinois. He had the financial capability to fund our growth. Our first year, we sold $600,000 and the second year $1,500,000. *We were "off to the races."* Harry was primarily involved with the banking and financials, and I ran everything else. I hired some really good guys who certainly contributed to the success we had: Bruce Jarzmik was a former "head hunter," Don Wilson was a salesman with Carburundum, Gene Nickleman, Don's brother-in-law who moved up from Bloomington, Illinois, and Doug Stein, my son, who did a great job with the Food Brokers. *We had a great team.*

Don Wilson's hiring is a story in itself. Don went to an employment agency in Naperville looking for a job. His interview was with Lola. Lola called me about him, and he didn't even realize that she was my wife until his interview with me. I eventually had to let Don go, but we were still friends. He recommended that his brother-in-law (Gene Nickleman) replace him. Gene and Bruce dealt with our non-food reps. But because of growth, we needed someone to work with Food

Brokers. That's where Doug entered the scene. Doug worked with food brokers across the United States and brought our business from almost nothing to over three million. I got great reports from the brokers regarding Doug, which made me very proud to be his dad.

Hal Stein

Stein heads plastics firm

Hal Stein of Naperville has been named president of North American Plastics, an Aurora-based manufacturer of plastic trash and lawn bags.

Previously a division manager for Union Carbide, Stein joined North American Plastics as a sales manager in 1972. He served as vice president and executive vice president before his recent appointment to president.

North American Plastics maintains production facilities in Aurora and Tustin, Calif., with nationwide distribution of its products. Among his other duties, Stein will be heading up the new expansion program which is being planned.

His civic involvements include membership in the Housewares Club of Chicago, the board of directors for the University of Dubuque's Alumni Association and the board of directors for the Woods of Bailey Hobson Homeowners Association.

20

Company Outings

Although we worked hard, a lot of fun was always tossed into the mix. We had a National Sale's Meeting every year at the time of the Housewares Show where we entertained our reps and our customers at the same time. Here are just a few of our many company outings:

We took 100 people to a White Sox game. We rode the double decker buses and went on to serve lunch in the picnic area where we met Minnie Minoso (famous Sox ball player). We also had our name shown on the scoreboard. *Everybody got a kick out of the fact that I bought out the peanut vendor and threw bags of peanuts to our guests (as well as many others).*

We went to the Planetarium where we held a private company showing. Afterward, we went on to the 95th floor of the Hancock Building for dinner (fancy place).

We had a cruise on Lake Michigan.

We took everyone to the Horse Races at Maywood Park. There was a special race in our name and then we awarded a special trophy to the winner after the race.

Bruce, Don, Gene, and Bill Sanders (Comptroller) and I played Liar's Poker at lunch, which was a lot of fun.

One summer I hired Chris and her friend to paint different things at the Plant. She had to climb up ladders and wear a plastic apron in an area that had high heat temperatures from the machines. It was a good experience for her—especially because she then found out that she definitely did *not* want to be a plastic worker in a factory.

21

Innovations

Through some contacts, I found out about the fact that Archer Daniels Midland (world's largest corn processor) was making a cornstarch that could be used with plastic to make it biodegradable. I thought we could use this technology because micro-organisms would attack the cornstarch in a landfill and break up the plastic in the process. In other words, they would disintegrate. *This innovative idea received a great deal of press. In fact, I was on the McNeil Lehre Report once—a nationally syndicated television show.*

Eventually, my great idea was stymied. Environmentalists thought the bags would not be recyclable due to the cornstarch. We did have some other ideas, however, that set us apart from our competition. When I first started the company, I thought we could be successful by offering big chains a private-label product with their name on it. This way, they could compete with well-advertised national brands. They could then sell an equal product at a much lower price while still promoting their own name.

We were the first company to offer bags on a roll. This cut the cost of production, and it also made the product much easier to dispense. At that time, "Glad Bags" and Hefty Bags" were only sold in a box that dispensed them one at a time. We also came up with some promotions that were unique. We gave away "free bags" where the consumer had to send in a coupon to get his money back. By the time the postage was paid, it really wasn't worthwhile. Our redemption was less that 3%, but it gained us 73 new retail customers. *All in all, we had a lot of fun trying innovative promotions.*

I always had good relationships with the workers at North American Plastics, and I think you could say we had a mutual respect. Several months before I actually decided to leave the company, I became quite involved with their protection. At this time, the Union had stepped in to attempt to organize our Plant. Their promise was to more than double everyone's wages. Hearing this, I ran a campaign (with an interpreter) that lasted three weeks. I met with the employees of three shifts (24 hours). During that time, I explained to them that it would be impossible for North American Plastics to continue its business with such a drastic increase in expenses. Instead, I proposed other benefits that would better suit the company's financial possibilities. I suggested Christmas bonuses, birthday celebrations for everyone, and the opportunity to cultivate a vegetable garden on the property. The night before the big vote, the Union could see that they only had five votes in their favor. There were 125 votes against them. Luckily, the Union pulled the petition.

When I left North American Plastics, the employees signed a petition for me to return. Later, one of the ladies gave me the plaque of a saint that she had prayed to in my behalf. *I felt honored that the employees really cared for me.*

22

After NAPCO

After leaving NAPCO, Gene Nickleman, Doug, and I worked for Chicago Transparent for one year. After that, I invested in a company called Laser Fab and became their President. The idea was to cut plastic pieces for various industries with a laser cutter. The company turned out to be short lived because all the potential customers that had been promised by the founder had vanished into thin air. After Laser Fab, I volunteered my time at Fox Tech which was a school for high-school aged boys who were high risk students. Some of them were even destined to spend their time in jail. We worked with the premise that they needed to learn a skill that could be done in a hands-on manner while they met the goal of obtaining a GED. We ran a wood shop that made futons that were popular products at that time. At the same time, they worked on their high school studies. I was their business manager and really enjoyed this work. Following this work, I became the CEO of Retirement Resorts for which I made a small investment. We did the marketing for upscale retirement locations around the world. It was also interesting work, and we had some good financial success.

In 1984 (after Lola's death), I joined a small Lutheran church back in Naperville. It was called The Good Shepherd and it had 130 members. I became very active, and was involved to the point of participating on the Church Council. As a group, we decided that we all had the goal of expanding the church by building a whole new structure. We had set the bar very high with the projection of a 2.2 million project. So, my committee rolled up our sleeves to raise as much as we could. The first contribution was $360,000 that was raised by my committee. Then came a large contribution ($250,000) from a couple in Ohio. I was so enthused that I paid for the purchase of a new organ (anonymously). I did this in honor of my deceased wife, Lola. It was such an honor to have been a part of the inception of this new church in Naperville. Today, the Good Shepherd Church has a membership of over 5,000 people. I have stayed very close to the Senior Pastors, Greg Wenhold and Gary Olson, and in fact, they married Mary and me in 2013.

$$23$$

Three Beautiful Children

Kim

Kimberley Ann Stein was born On August 31, 1959 in Indianapolis. I've got so many fond memories of Kim since the day she was born. Of course, she was a totally adorable little girl. She and her sister (and Lola) always seemed to have the "specialty" of liking to shop. They bought clothes "on approval" that they thought were in style at the time. Many times, I'd find clothes hanging in closets and they would say, *"Oh those have been here for months!"* Grandma Stegner always encouraged the shopping, too. She loved to buy clothes for Lola and the girls, so it was only natural that Kim and Chris would follow suit.

When Kim was a little girl, we had the fun of participating in Indian Princess. Together we *were Big Rock and Little Stone.* We took lots of photos to remember the good times dressing up and playing the role together.

Kim decided to go to my alma mater, The University of Dubuque. In my eyes, she really seemed to blossom while she was there. Kim had her 19th birthday soon after she arrived at school, so we sent her a big birthday cake. Somehow, the bakery made a mistake and sent her two big cakes. *I don't know if that won her more friends, but she certainly was popular at her new school.*

Kim was a pompom girl for the University football team and was really good at it. Her mother and I were so very proud of her when we watched her performance at the Homecoming Game! *It was really impressive.* Kim continued to meet people and was very popular among her classmates. She even joined the best sorority on campus. To this day, I don't know how she managed to date boys from both the football and basketball teams. She exuded self-confidence. Kim had so much fun at Dubuque that she lasted only two years there. She returned home and went on to attend Robert Morris College where she really found her niche. She was accomplished in all the secretarial areas. Kim landed some good jobs including 84 Lumber, Bell Labs, and Majors Marketing Research.

Kim eventually met a great guy named Bruno Fussel. He was the perfect complement for her. He was even-keeled, adored my daughter, and was a good provider. He owned a vacuum cleaner store. Bruno was born in Germany and typically was very disciplined. His mother, Maria, told many stories about how badly their people had been treated first by the Nazis and then by the Russians. (She was a wonderful and loving person.) I must say that Kim and Bruno's wedding was one of the highlights of my life. We held the wedding at Our Saviors Lutheran Church and the reception was at Stouffers in Oak Brook. I'll never forget Stella dancing the Hokey Pokey like a teenager. The rehearsal dinner was at Willoway Manor in Oak Brook. I read a poem and Uncle Doug gave Kim a football helmet in memory of her childhood exploits as a football player when we spent Thanksgivings at his home in Louisville. Kim and Bruno gave me three beautiful grandsons: Bradley Allen Fussel (1986), Ryan Wilhelm Fussel (1989), and Christopher Douglas Fussel (1995). I'm so proud of them.

Doug

On May 27, 1962, Douglas Wesley Stein was born in Indianapolis at the Coleman Hospital. Lola and I were thrilled to now have both a boy and a girl! Doug was named after his Uncle Doug Stegner, and Wesley after Lola's father.

We moved to Naperville when Doug was young (three or four). There was a little girl who lived across the street named Patty LaRue who became his best friend. He used to come outside in the winter wearing summer clothes, and Patty would send him back in the house to wear something warmer. *They were really cute together.* We also had a big time with birthday celebrations at our house. Once we had a sheet draped over a clothesline in the basement, and the kids fished for prizes with a fishing pole. They dropped the line over the sheet and I was there on the other side to attach a prize onto the hook! *I think I liked it as much as they did!*

Doug and I were really into in the Indian Guides. We were *Big Bow and Little Arrow*. I remember going to George Williams College in the winter to sled and stay overnight in their dorms. We also marched together in the Memorial Day Parade with the cool totem pole that we made. We wore feathers and vests. *What a sight.* Doug was also in the Boy Scouts and I was Camping Chairman. One February, we camped in a cave in Wisconsin. That night, I woke up and heard a symphony of snoring. Every sound resonated with the domed ceiling.

Doug tried out for Little League and made the *"Majors"* as a ten-year old. This was a really big deal, as there were only two ten-year olds on each team. The coaches drafted players based on their ability. *Just like the Major Leagues!* In Doug's first game in the Majors, the coach told him to bunt when it was his turn at bat. Well, the pitch smacked him right on his finger and he needed three stitches. *What a start!* Lola, Kim, Chris, and I all went to every game. If Doug got a hit, we rewarded everyone with a trip to Dairy Queen for a treat. The girls liked the baseball games, but I think they had secret crushes on the coach, too (Tom Lubke). At age 13, Doug graduated up into the Pony League (13 and 14 year-olds), and I became manager with Al Kennedy as the coach. Al was a very good coach (he played in college). Doug played 2nd base and he was a good hitter. Doug probably got the short end of it, however, since I wanted to make sure that every boy got equal playing time—even if they weren't so good. *Doug was a good sport about it and never complained.*

Doug bought an old car for $750, and the deal was that he had to pay half from money he had earned (K Mart Toys, JoJo's Restaurant bus boy, and others). The car needed a lot of bodywork, so Doug took it apart and we had Bondo all over the house.

In high school, Doug played on the tennis team. We also had a discussion one night about his grades. Doug said, *"C is average, that's all I need."* I said, *"If you get C's in high school, you won't do any better in college."* Then and there, Doug and I drew up a contract saying that if Doug got less than a B average in college, he would owe me $500 and if he graduated with a B or better, I would pay him $500. *It's the best contract I've ever made and the best $500 I have ever spent!*

Speaking of college, Doug chose Carthage on the shores of Lake Michigan in Wisconsin. In Doug's senior year, he was President of the fraternity. The fraternity had a problem since they had a forbidden beer party on campus. They were in trouble with the President of the school, and the fraternity was actually kicked off the campus. They asked me to write a letter to the President about the situation. He did write back and was very kind and understanding but just wanted the fraternity to live by the rules.

Doug worked every summer starting at age sixteen. He worked at the jobs I mentioned earlier as well as one summer that he worked for me at the apartment complex that Lola and I owned. We had 36 Units, so we needed a manager. One of the managers we had was a single gal who had served as an assistant manager. When we fired the manager (alcoholic), I asked her to step up and take his place. I told her I wanted to have her bonded because she would be handling cash payments. The next day, she told me that she could not be bonded because she had a record as a "hooker." I hired her anyway since she was very good with the tenants. Anyway, Doug painted apartments with her all summer. She eventually took off after 6 months with one of the tenants. Our next managers were Jack and Svea McCall, an older couple, who settled things down until I sold the apart-

Hal, Kim, Doug, Chris

Doug's graduation

Chris, Andy, and baby Caitlyn

Doug and Jean's wedding

*All three children
and their families*

Letter from Christina

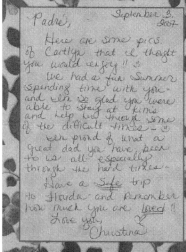

Padré,   September 3, 2007

Here are some pics. of Caitlyn that I thought you would enjoy!! 😊

We had a fun summer spending time with you— and I'm so glad you were able to stay at Kim's and help us through some of the difficult times— 😊

I'm proud of what a great dad you have been to us all— especially through the hard times—

Have a safe trip to Florida and remember how much you are loved !!

Love you,
Christina

Doug's baseball team

*Doug and Hal (me) the
day Kennedy was born*

Kim's wedding   *Kim the Pom Pom Girl*

Dancing with daughter, Kim

Kim and Bruno   *L to R: Chris, Doug, Kennedy Kim, and Christopher*

All the married couples

Me, my Dad, Harry and our first grandson, Brad

Three Beautiful Children and their Families

ments after about seven years. The apartments were a great investment—I ended up with 15 times my return.

Doug married an intelligent, beautiful girl named Jean McGould. They met at what was called the world's largest block party. Apparently when they first met, they knew that something very special was in the air. Jean was a computer consultant and quite a runner. She was athletic enough to have sponsors for racing competitions. Their wedding was held on a sunny spring day in Wheaton, Illinois. Her parents, Chuck and Barbara McGould really created a fantastic wedding event. The priest who conducted the services was a real card, and he had a beautiful singing voice. I had the honor of reading a poem (at the reception) I wrote for them. It was pretty funny—"It's All in the Genes!" I pointed out that the bride's name is Jean, Lola's middle name is Jean, and my middle name is Gene. By the way, their rehearsal dinner was at The Braxton in Oak Brook. It had a beautiful domed ceiling with the unique feature of a tremendous echo throughout the room. It was an event that I will always remember. Doug and Jean had four fabulous children named Theodore Douglas Stein (1998), Truman Douglas Stein (2000), Kennedy Marie Stein (2002), and Woodrow Douglas Stein (2003). They are all such great kids!

Chris

Chris was born in Memphis, Tennessee and that's why we gave her the middle name *Lee* (Robert E. Lee). So, on January 4, 1967, we added our family's youngest—Christina Lee Stein. She was a real joy as a baby. At the time, we hired a maid to help around the house and to take care of Chris while Lola shopped and ran errands. Hattie loved taking care of Chris.

Chris really came into her own when we moved to Naperville. She had a lot of friends and seemed to be the leader of the pack. I remember one night when she and her girl friends ventured into Chicago (by car) at 10 o'clock at night in the fog. Later, they told me that they had actually taken a carriage ride.

One night, Chris and her friends got the idea to test what it would be like to sleep all night in a car. They wanted to be relatively safe, so they parked outside Kim and Bruno's condo. During the night, the local police roused them out of their sleep. Chris immediately gave them Kim's telephone number, so Kim was the next to be woken up. Kim was embarrassed, but no damage was done.

Chris and I participated in Indian Guides for three years. We were *Little Cloud and Big Thunder*. That was a really fun time for everyone. I also have a memory of the night our family camped out at Ray Knudson's farm. We had a fire roaring and we roasted large steaks from Ray's stock. Anyway, the cows were *mooing* during the night, so this made Chris wake me up every hour with the excuse of taking her to the potty.

Kim and Doug thought that Chris was really cute when she was angry. Basically, they thought up things that might provoke her so they could catch another glimpse of her *cuteness!* Once she got mad and tossed a bench down the stairs. *Really cute!*

Chris went to my alma mater (as did Kim). When Chris arrived at Dubuque, she met her athletic African-American roommate who smoked and had a group of friends in the room. Chris felt like the odd one out in this atmosphere, so after just a few days she called to say that she wanted to come home. Doug and I picked her up, and on the way home we reminded her that she would now need to get a job and move in with Pat's kids. *The next day, she opted to return to Dubuque and stayed there for the next four years.*

Chris eventually met a wonderful guy named Andy Drone. They met at the University of Dubuque (my alma mater). Their wedding was at Good Shepard Lutheran Church in Naperville with a reception at White Eagle Country Club. Chris had been dating Andy for some time, and we all hoped that they would someday be married. Chris always had her heart set on White Eagle Country Club for a wedding reception. Even though they were not even engaged, Kim, Chris, and I went ahead and inquired about potential timing. White Eagle Country Club was known to have a one-year waiting list. Aha! They had a cancellation for November 17th. So, we booked it. When Andy asked her (finally) to marry him, Chris told him that her dad had already booked November 17th for their wedding. "What?" he said. "That's deer hunting season opening day in Wisconsin!" But since the show must go on, they had to keep the booking. Andy's family was not thrilled to hear that he was to be married on the biggest day of their hunting season. There were eleven children in his family, so the disappointment ran deep. They reluctantly did attend the wedding festivities, but wore their orange deer-hunting garb to the rehearsal dinner. To apologize for the change of their family (hunting) plans, we all decided to add to the fun (another practical joke). At the wedding, everyone was elegantly dressed in tuxedos. On cue, all the guys opened their jackets to expose bright orange-colored hunting vests! Seemed like everyone quickly forgot about the hunting! But then came the clincher! His brother got us back again! When Andy and Chris were kneeling at the alter during the ceremony, his brother had written on the bottom of Andy's shoe, "I got my doe!" In a fast-forward to later years, Chris and Andy gave me a beautiful granddaughter named Caitlyn Kimberly Drone (2003). She is a joy!

24

Thanksgiving Fun

Every Thanksgiving, Lola and I bundled up our family for a visit to her brother's house in Louisville, Kentucky. Doug Stegner was a fun brother-in-law, and always showed us a great time. Doug owned a mansion across from Cherokee Park. Before Thanksgiving dinner, it was a tradition to play a game (competitive) of touch football. One side had Doug Stegner, Kim, Missy, and myself. The other side had Doug's three boys, Doug Stein, and Beth. We knew that our secret weapon was the fact that the boys argued with each other about everything—who was the quarterback, who was the ball carrier, etc. *This was a big distraction for them and we counted on it serving us well.*

A time limit was set for the game. (Doug Stegner was timekeeper.) He conveniently stopped the clock when our team was ahead and then he called the game. *The boys, Greg, Brad, and Jeff still complain (to this day) about how time stood still 40 years ago!* We all still remember that my daughter, Kim (the least athletic) scored the winning touchdown one year!

While we were playing football, the women (Lola and Alice) were drinking and making dinner (in that order it seems). No one generally ate before 10 PM even though we were all starving. *The women were happily in the bag!*

Thanksgiving family reunion at the Stegners in Louisville, Kentucky (2004)

25

More Trips to Louisville

One year, we decided to invite some good friends to visit Doug and Alice in Louisville. Everyone was ready for some fun. Bill and Connie Conklin, Bob and Arlen Jambor, and Dale and Sandy Johnson joined Lola and me for a weekend. We all decided to go to the racetrack in Keenland, Kentucky (near Lexington).

I thought I knew something about handicapping the races, so I gave Dale some tips on which horses were the favorites in each race. It turned out that I wasn't as good as I thought. In fact, we lost almost every race. It also turned out that two very large black men standing behind Dale had a question or two. *"Who is that guy? (referring to me) What's he thinking? We've been betting on his advice and now we've lost our shirts!"* The next day we went to Churchill Downs (home of the Kentucky Derby) and we all did much better!

26

A Letter From Heaven

When I was 40 years old, I found a mysterious letter. This letter left me speechless, and to this day, I cannot put my feelings into words. It was a godsend. Webster's Dictionary defines the word godsend as a *desirable or needed thing or event that comes unexpectedly*. I think they should change this definition to "*Hal's Letter From Heaven*."

After Aunt Bernice (my mother's sister) died, I had some duties to perform as the executor of her will. It was such a sad time—Aunt Bernice had loved me unconditionally throughout my childhood, and I felt the same for her. One day, I was searching for some legal papers in her desk drawer when I saw a cursive letter written in faded pencil. My heart pounded, and I broke out in a cold sweat. I could not believe what I had found. I was holding a letter that was written to me by my mother on the day before she died. I held my breath. A small miracle was in my hand.

The letter she wrote to me carved an imprint in my heart. It touched me deeply and served as a turning point in my life. It was a blessing and a sign that my mother would always be with me. *To this day, my mother's letter is one of my most cherished possessions.*

Letter from Heaven: Mom's letter

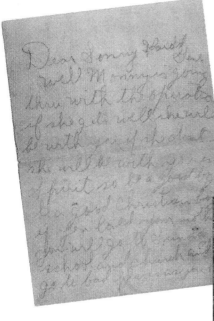

Aunt Bernice a big
part of my life

Aunt Bernice and Uncle
LaVerne's wedding

Aunt Bernice and Uncle LaVerne

27

Green Bay Packers with the Guys

When you think about it, just about every football fan in the world would like to visit Lambeau Field—home of the Green Bay Packers. Even Bears fans (like myself) were intrigued by the Packer's history. My good friend, Dale Johnson, had four season tickets for the Packers since 1963. This was almost impossible to imagine! All of our friends wanted to be invited, so we more or less lined up for the fun. I really cherished the times that I was included with Dale, Bill Conklin, Bob Jambor, and all.

Once, we left on a Saturday so we could visit all of Dale's haunts along the way. It was my first game, so the guys had to "break me in" as a sort of Packer initiation. I wore a tee shirt with the name ROOKIESTEIN on the back, and was expected to make the drinks and perform other servant's chores. During the game, Bob Jambor went back to his car to retrieve his sunglasses but never came back. He had gotten lost in the parking lot! (The next time we went to a game, we gave him a ball of string and connected it to his pants.)

We all stayed at the Titletown Motel so we could be right in the middle of all the action. Prior to the game, a TV crew was canvassing the tailgate party when they spotted our group and thought we were the life of the party! Dale was interviewed as our "spokesperson." Lo and behold—that night we were featured on the local TV news!

And that's just a sample of all the fun we had at Packer games. I really enjoyed them.

Green Bay Packer Trip L to R: Dale Johnson, Bob Jambor,
Roger Letchworth, Bill Conklin, and Joe Grier.

28

Florida on my Mind

After many good years in different parts of the country, retirement was softly calling my name. The most logical place to explore was Florida—the *Sunshine State*. I had spent many good times in Florida and had learned to love it there. My good friend, Dale Johnson, had moved to Florida and was encouraging me to do the same. I thought about the wonderful Christmas holidays on Sanibel Island, the great times in Naples, and the many retirement communities visited. Florida was hard to resist.

Let's flash back to Sanibel Island, Florida in 1986 when our family spent the Christmas week there. We had a fabulous time. Kim and Bruno gave me a small doll for my Christmas gift. As I peeled off the wrapping paper, I was not sure how to react. I just couldn't figure out why in the world they would give me a doll. I heard them chuckling. Then, it hit me! They announced that Kim was pregnant (with Brad) and I still can feel the joy of that moment. Believe it or not, I kept that doll and years later, Brad and his wife, Tara, gave it to Kim and her family as an announcement that their daughter (Jocelyn) was on her way. I still have the doll for the next announcements! Sanibel holds such strong memories for me. I visited there two more times and almost bought a condo in 1987.

Several miles down the road from Sanibel, the allure of another beautiful Florida spot hit me - Naples. I was getting very "Florida serious" at this point, so I put a down a deposit on a high-rise condominium to be built at a later date. It was 1989 and my accountant advised me not to go through with the purchase. He felt that it was not financially feasible, so I withdrew my offer. *Today, that condo is valued at over one million dollars!*

Not to be discouraged, I kept looking at different places in Florida for an eventual move. Then, in 2000, I saw what The Villages had to offer and I thought it was a little bit of Heaven. The Villages/Del Webb area has been home since then, and I have never regretted my decision.

29

Invitation To France

During the "Florida shopping time" in October of 1990, I received an interesting invitation in the mail. It was written in French (**Vous** êtes **cordialemente invité au marriage...**). It had all the markings of a must-do experience. My friend, Joe Grier, had invited me to attend his son's (Josh) wedding in Paris! Now, I knew that this wedding was going to be quite an affair since the father of the bride was a big international Armenian lawyer. The bride and groom were also lawyers and represented some very interesting clients (to say the least). *How could I say no to such an event?*

Well, my first taste of Paris was not particularly good. People were pushing and shoving each other to board the train, so I instinctively pushed back. When I did this, someone took the opportunity to pick my pocket. I saw the guy who did it, and I called out to him, "Hey!" He gestured back - that gesture saying, "Are you crazy?" Joe also caught a guy trying to put his hand in his pocket, but in this case, nothing was lost. Things went fast, and we had to move on. Anyway, Joe and I loved walking the streets and looking at all the beautiful architecture. We even climbed up the narrow stairway of the Notre Dame Cathedral.

Josh's wedding was just as spectacular as we expected. The guests were the "cream" of society. There were lawyers, judges, bankers, and so forth. We enjoyed a seven-course dinner with an eleven-piece band. In the middle of it all, we were surprised to be entertained by a belly dancer, an Armenian custom. Oh, and did I mention that the whole affair was televised?

After the thrill of this amazing wedding, we made plans to cross the Channel to England. Joe and I made reservations to take the train (or so we thought) from Paris to Charlet, France where we would catch the Hover Craft to Dover, England. When we arrived at the train, we were told that our tickets were for the bus—not the train. Fortunately, the bus station was only a few blocks away. Since we had so many bags, we hired a valet (with a dolly) to take our bags to the bus depot. When we arrived at the bus depot, we asked the valet to give the station-master our tickets. The valet said, *"Oh no. I've lost your tickets!"* Dramatically, he pulled his pant pockets inside out to make certain we understood his point. *No tickets.* Then, out of nowhere, a swarthy man pushed us aside saying, *"I found these tickets on the street. Are they yours?"* Relief. We quickly boarded the bus with a driver who looked like Charles de Gaulle, which makes a good (but impossible) story. No sooner were we seated, before I noticed a young couple going through the exact same "lost ticket" problem that we had just experienced. From my window, I could see the tickets lying on the ground behind them. Wanting to be a Good Samaritan, I got off the bus and retrieved their tickets. With that, "Charles de Gaulle" took off with the three of us running along and pounding on the side of the bus for him to stop. After the (obvious) fun of watching us sprint for six blocks, he brought the bus to a stop so we could get back on. *And, yes, we all saw that silly smirk on his face when he swung open the doors.*

The rest of the trip was lots of fun and relatively uneventful (of mishaps). Our Hover Ride was great and we really enjoyed everything about London. We stayed in a quaint Bed and Breakfast (one bathroom for every six guests) and really got to know the area. *All in all, it was a trip to remember.*

30

A Hal-Mary Meeting

My daughter, Chris, told me that she thought I needed someone special again in my life and that it didn't matter at all that I was 79 years old. She took the liberty of signing me up for a Christian Mingle Website. Well, the first week, I spotted an attractive lady named Mary Robinson on the site, so I went ahead and gave her a call. I was happy that she answered my call, but was disappointed that she immediately said she would have to call me back in one hour. After I didn't hear back from her, I tried her again, but she was still on the other line. My first instinct was, "Forget this!" But, Mary's information on the website had intrigued me (she was fun-loving and an excellent golfer), so I called her back three days later. This time she answered and agreed to meet the following Monday after she attended a neighborhood golf outing. We met in a hotel, and when I walked in, there must have been 50 people in the lobby staring at me. I later found out that they were all primed to "size me up." I must have passed their approval!

After a short time, I invited Mary to attend my 80th birthday party where I had invited my whole family and 90 of my closest friends. She said she would love to, but she and her family were going to the mountains in Tennessee and that she might not be back in time. She said she would really try to be there. The good news is that she did make it to the party for the last hour. She was able to meet my family and friends for the first time. I guess you could say this was a kind of "audition" –just as I had previously with her friends. Things went really great and our families have been close ever since.

Mary was born in Mays Landing, New Jersey (Mary Louise Aurelio), where she lived until she was 15 years old. At that time, her family moved to West Palm Beach, Florida. She studied nursing and became an RN, specializing as a psych nurse. Later, she owned and operated an Assisted Living Center in Panama City, Florida. Happily, Mary always found time to perfect her golf game along with the many friendships that go along with the sport! Mary's son, Richard Todd Martin (1970), and his wife, Holly, have two boys named Gavin Thomas Martin

(2003), and Rylan Todd Martin (2008). Her daughter, Julie Elizabeth Barrentine (1964), and her husband, Rex, have two daughters named Brooke Elizabeth Jett (1989), and Bailee Alyse Barrentine (1996). They were all part of the celebration of our new beginning together.

31

A New Beginning

Mary and I were married on July 13, 2013 at my Lutheran Church in Naperville, Illinois. Two Pastors wanted to participate, and Pastor Gary Olson's wife performed as the soloist. The reception was held in Kim's back yard. Mary's children prepared the food and my granddaughter, Caitlyn, played the violin. Truly a great time for all!

Since then, Mary and I have enjoyed so many wonderful family gatherings. We have taken several cruises, traveled around the United States, and hosted many parties. We are involved in church activities and have remained active on an ongoing daily basis. Last year (2017) was momentous because both Mary and I became great-grandparents. Mary's granddaughter, Brooke and her husband, Kenny Jett had a little boy named Benson. My grandson and his wife (Brad and Tara Fussel) had a little girl named Jocelyn. *There are many birthday parties to look forward to!*

Wedding photo

Mary and Hal

A night at the Philharmonic Gala

32

Honduras

Looking back, we all remember a horrific time in United State's history. It was September 11, 2001, the day an Islamic extremist group (al-Quaeda) hijacked four airplanes and carried out suicide attacks against the U.S. Two of the planes were flown into the twin towers in New York City, and a third plane hit the Pentagon, just outside of Washington, D.C. Later, a fourth plane crashed in a field in Pennsylvania. Almost 3,000 people were killed, and panic set in throughout the country. Five days later (Sunday, September 16, 2001), I attended church to pray for the victims and their families. After prayer, our Pastor mentioned that a group of 30 people had planned an upcoming mission trip to Honduras. The big question now was, "Would we still go?" We took a poll, and half the group decided to back out for obvious reasons. Everyone was fearful of flying during this tumultuous time. When it was time for my vote, I said, "Maybe next year I will go." So what finally happened? The next thing I knew, I had seven shots and I was on my way to Honduras!

Now fast-forward to 2013. I was telling my grandson, Christopher, some stories about my Honduras trip when he said, "I'd love to do that! I'd go there if I could!" His enthusiasm really impressed me. I spontaneously said, "Well then, you've got a deal!" Mary chimed in with, "Well, I'm a nurse. I'll go, too!" We decided to go to Honduras in October, and since it was only three months after our wedding, we called it our "honeymoon!"

So, the three of us boarded a 972- mile flight to Honduras, a Spanish Island in Central America. We arrived after an all-night flight with all kinds of medical supplies, reading glasses, and other sundries. We stayed in the Mission House, which was by no means fancy—bunk beds, cold showers, and the bare necessities. The first day, we took school busses to a small church that had been transformed into a triage hospital. We were shocked to see people lined up (as far as we could see) for the first medical help that many had ever experienced. Christopher was given his first job. He had the task (along with some other men) of pouring a cement floor in a lady's house. This was a lady who had prayed for years to improve her dirt floor that had bugs crawling all over it. Mary and I were given the job of distributing medical supplies that were prescribed by the doctors.

On the second day, Christopher was given the job of running the defractor eye machine. The machine indicated what eye glasses were needed for each patient. Christopher was like the Pied Piper of Honduras—all the little kids followed him all over. His next job was working with the Honduran dentist on staff. The dentist said to him, "How would you like to pull some teeth?" That was quite a question! Christopher ended up pulling four teeth, which was pretty traumatic. We ended up treating and praying for 2,800 people and gave away 1,500 pair of reading glasses.

Christopher was like a Rock Star from the first night that we all told the group why we were there. He said, "I'm here to find God." This simple statement both stunned and impressed everyone. No one expected a young guy to say such a thing. *The bottom line of this whole time in Honduras was that Christopher said it was the best time of his life, and Mary and I got off to a wonderful marriage experience as a couple.*

Mary and I had a breakfast to raise funds for our mission trip. We had 54 people.

We face painted and talked about Jesus with the kids in Honduras.

Christopher worked with the Honduran dentist when he pulled four teeth.

33

Keeping in Touch

I have a tremendous respect for young people today as they are faced with complicated technology and temptations that we never knew. It's important for adults to keep in touch with young people for the sole reason of just "being there" for them and offering whatever guidance we can. My grandchildren are one of my life's top priorities, and I love communicating with them. One special thing that I do for them is to send what I call A *Weekly Life Lesson* to think about. They look forward to receiving this every Sunday, and have expressed their gratitude over and over. Here are a few examples of *Life's Lessons:*

Learn to play and appreciate good music.
Be humble. Even though I know you are great.
If you aim at nothing, you'll hit it every time.
Who did I smile at today, and who did I make feel good today?
A friend is someone who is walking in when everyone else is walking out.
A person who rolls up his sleeves seldom loses his shirt.
Life is not a dress rehearsal. What you do every day is important.
Find a need and fill it.
Readers are leaders. Learn to speed read.
Life is like riding a bicycle. You don't fall off unless you stop pedaling.
Success is a choice; failure is not an option.
Don't sweat the small stuff.
We become what we think about.
Don't confuse activity with achievement.
The longest journey starts with the first steps.
Attitude is everything.
Today is the first day of the rest of your life.

Our wedding 2013

Our combined Family 2013 at get together for Christmas in Panama City Beach, FL

34

Gratitude For Life's Lessons

I'd like to share some words that I received via e-mail that show the gratitude for my efforts with Life's Lessons to my grandchildren. All of the children have told me how much they have appreciated these words of wisdom. I also think the lessons are especially important (to them) because these are words from their grandfather.

"Dear Papa, I am writing this letter to you because I want you to understand how much I appreciate all that you have done for me. So much that I can't decide where to even begin. Fore one thing you have helped me to find a career that I could be interested in. Having you by my side makes me feel like I can do anything I set my mind to. You have taken the time to visit colleges that I was interested in. With your help I found just the right college for me. I can only hope that one day I will be a successful as you were and are. You are an inspiration. I enjoy going to eat with you on these special occasions because you are very wise and you know about everything I am going through. I feel like I can always come to you no matter what the subject and you will be understanding and you will tell me the right path I should be taking. One day I hope that I will be as successful as you and be able to show you everything that you have shown me. I want to show you that all the time you spent on me will pay off. Papa, I appreciate everything you have done for me and I appreciate the times you have been there for me." Love, Ryan

"I love you too, Papa. I really like that one. I want you to know that one of the highlights of my day is when I get a text like this from you. I've saved most if not all of these because you have an incredible amount of wisdom papa and I want you to know that I really mean that and I value it greatly. You are an idol of mine and I respect you more than you know. With every fiber of my being I mean it when I say that I could have not asked for a better grandfather. You have a wealth of knowledge that is very valuable to me and I wish to learn all of it from you. You are truly the greatest grandfather one can ask for and I really do mean that. I absolutely love you papa and I could not be more grateful for your wisdom and guidance. It's something I need and I will never forget any of it. I love you papa and I couldn't possibly be more proud to call you my grandfather." Love, Christopher

Christopher's baptism

Dancing with granddaughter Caitlyn

Kim, Ryan, Christopher, Bruno, Brad at my 80th birthday celebration

35

Ancestry.Com

When I decided to write a book of memoirs, I thought it would be fitting to include a "proper" list of my heritage. Ancestry.com is quite the craze right now, so I wanted to give it a go. I mailed in a saliva sample, and the results were interesting. Remember, the Vikings were from Norway and they really circled the globe. Also, remember that Jesus was a Jew and God called the Jews his "chosen people." *I feel honored.*

41% European Jewish
29% Scandinavian (Norway)
19% Great Briton
03% West Europe
02% Italy
02% Finland and Russia
01% Native American
02% Caucasian

Brad, Ryan, and Joe the Cop

Truman celebrating my
80th with balloons!

L to R: (back) Brad, Ryan, Hal, Christopher,
(front) Teddy, Truman, Kennedy, Woodrow, and Caitlyn

36

Active At Eighty-six

Yes, I'm 86, but I can't wait to see what the future holds. *Thank you, God.* In times of need, I softly recite the 23rd Psalm and I meditate on the words. It's grace and mercy is so inspiring. *The Lord is my shepherd; I shall not want. He makes me lie down in green pastures. He leads me beside still waters. He restores my soul. He leads me in paths of righteousness for his name's sake. Even though I walk through the valley of the shadow of death, I will fear no evil, for you are with me; your rod and your staff, they comfort me. You prepare a table before me in the presence of my enemies; you anoint my head with oil; my cup overflows. Surely goodness and mercy shall follow me all the days of my life, and I shall dwell in the house of the Lord forever.* In my own words, *"Life is but a pit stop on the way to eternity."*

I am presently involved in the Garden Worship Center in Belleview, Florida. Norman Lee Schaffer is the Pastor and is a great inspiration to the congregation. It's a non-denominational church that started 8 years ago (2010) in a local shopping center. Now, Garden Worship Center has over 2,000 members and is growing every day. The Pastor asked me to be an Elder of the Church, and a true "elder" I am at the age of 86. I am involved in every aspect of the church including Newcomer's Brunch, Small Groups, Potluck Dinner Nights, and Men's Fellowship for which I am the leader. There are 25 men in the Fellowship Group, so when Norman first asked me to take charge of it, I really felt that I wasn't qualified. I said, *"I'm not a certified teacher, I'm not a scholar of the Bible, I'm not experienced with this."* Basically, I searched for any excuse I could think of. Anyway, Norman convinced me to give it a try. That was over a year ago, and I have seen some unbelievable growth in both myself and the other guys. I've seen several miracles among the men—positive changes—from health to social, marital, and even drug issues. Three men from prison ministry, plus ministry leaders (David St. Vincent and Dan Cagle) also attend the meetings. The transformation from them and the others has been very inspirational. It has been amazing to witness the bonding of this group of men from so many different walks of life. I feel blessed to be a part of it. God bless you all: Bob H., Carl, Don, Dave, Wade, Bob O., Bill, Eric, Bob C., Scott, Lou, Jerry D., John, Ray, Jerry B., Greg, Mike, Steve, Anthony, Damen, Buzz, and Austin.

I feel blessed to be a part of this group.

2016 Christmas cruise on the Oosterdam!
Harry and Donna Hayes, Dale and Jane Johnson,
Hal and Mary Stein, and Carole and Bill Kugelman

FINAL THOUGHTS

I thought it might be appropriate to end this book with a quick glance at my week. My wish is to encourage my family to stay active (and positive) as long as possible without letting age (as a number) interfere. So, here goes: Saturday I spoke at a friend's memorial. Sunday I was asked to usher at the 9AM, 11AM, and 5:30 PM church services. After the 11AM service, Pastor Norman Lee asked me to fill in for him at the Newcomer's Luncheon. Monday I took a cooking class. Tuesday I met to co-chair a big golf outing. Wednesday Mary and I attended a concert and C.D. Introduction. Thursday night I hosted a Men's Fellowship where 20 men meet to discuss pertinent thoughts and reflections. And then, of course, Friday I worked on my twenty- thousand word Memoir, ***Here's the Thing About It....*** I hope you all enjoy it. My son Doug just called and he said, *"Gosh Dad, most guys your age just sit around and watch TV all day!"*

Made in the USA
Columbia, SC
26 October 2023

24936953R00052